Baby Is Coming!

by

Ann M. Pearson

Illustrated by

DG

Copyright © 2018 Ann M. Pearson

All rights reserved.

No part of this publication may be reproduced or transmitted without permission.

ISBN: 978-1-948599-04-7
Thoughts to Pen Publishing, Mt. Dora, FL
https://thoughtstopenpublishing.com

~ Dedicated to my grandchildren ~

Mommy's tummy gets bigger and bigger
so Baby will soon be here.

Mommy and Daddy say things
will change a bit
as Baby's birth day nears.

Mommy and Daddy will go to the hospital when it is time for Baby to be born.

They will get the care they need and a blanket to keep Baby warm.

While they are gone I may be
at home with someone special:

Grandma or Grandpa or the girl next door.
OH! Maybe we will make cookies -

OR homemade pretzels!

They say Baby will sleep a lot.
We have a crib AND cradle.

Baby may prefer to be held...
even by me when I am able!

They say Baby will eat often
and in places we usually don't.

Baby might eat in the living room
or even **in a boat**?

They say Baby will cry
to get our attention -

To let us know it is time
to sleep, eat, or receive affection.

They say Baby will need
changes of diapers and clothes.

At times Baby will need to be bathed from head to toes!

They say we will still play with toys,
watch movies, and go walking.

Baby will tag along
and listen to our talking.

Things may change a bit with the arrival of Baby.

The best change will be adding Baby to our family.

My Special Memories of Baby

DATE	MEMORY

Made in the
USA
Middletown, DE